Lend a Hand

Girl-sized ways of helping others

by Apryl Lundsten

illustrated by Josée Masse

★ American Girl®

Published by American Girl Publishing, Inc.
Copyright © 2011 by American Girl, LLC

Questions or comments? Call 1-800-845-0005,
visit our Web site at **americangirl.com**, or write to
Customer Service, American Girl, 8400 Fairway Place, Middleton, WI 53562-0497.

Printed in China
11 12 13 14 15 16 17 18 19 LEO 10 9 8 7 6 5 4 3 2 1

All American Girl marks are trademarks of American Girl, LLC.

Editorial Development: Carrie Anton, Jessica Nordskog

Art Direction & Design: Lisa Wilber

Production: Tami Kepler, Sarah Boecher, Jeannette Bailey, Judith Lary

Illustrations: Josée Masse

Dear Reader,

If helping others is important to you, knowing where to start may be the tricky part. You don't have to change the whole world to make a difference. Start small by pitching in around the house, being an understanding friend, or helping a family friend with yard work. When you're ready and have your parent's permission, find bigger ways to give back by doing things such as feeding hungry people, caring for the sick, protecting wildlife, and so much more!

In this book, you'll find lots of ideas for little (and large) ways to make a difference at home, among your friends, in your community, and on the planet. You'll find ways you can help your family, care for animals, and raise money for important causes. You'll get tips on how to speak out about issues that matter to you. Plus, you'll meet girls just like you who are lending a hand, and get real advice about how you can do it.

The best thing about lending a hand is what giving gives **you**: confidence, a feeling of being needed, a sense of pride and accomplishment, new friends, and fun.

So roll up your sleeves, turn the page, and get ready to make your world a better place—one small act at a time!

Your friends at American Girl

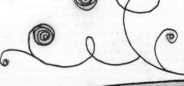

Helpful Ways

Do

Look for ways to **volunteer** your time and energy by doing things like putting groceries away at home, bringing dessert to a neighbor, raking your grandparents' yard, or being a good listener to a friend.

Give

Donate your old clothes, toys, books, and other items for a great way to give back—and clean out your closet!

Earn

Raise money to help your school, local animal shelter, community center, state park, or other organization pay for things it needs.

Say

Speak out about things you care about. You can teach those around you why it's important to save energy and recycle plastic bottles. You can also stand up for those who can't stand up for themselves, like animals.

Volunteer

There are all kinds of ways to lend your time. Here are some examples:

Take cookies to a firehouse or police station to let those workers know how much you appreciate their service.

Make a card for new neighbors to welcome them to the block.

Help watch the younger kids at a church day care.

Pull weeds from your grandmother's yard.

Make breakfast or lunch for your younger siblings.

Leave a thank-you note for your mail carrier, wishing him or her a great day.

Pet-sit for your friends and family members.

Raise awareness

Want your voice to be heard? Try these ideas:

- Give a speech about an important issue at school, church, or a parents' group, or to clubs you belong to.

- Work with a parent to write your own blog or create a Web site where you give the facts, details, and other information about a cause you're passionate about.

- With permission from Mom or Dad, make a video about your cause and post it online.

- Start a nature club with friends. Hold meetings to share information and talk about things like endangered species or wilderness areas that need to be preserved or restored.

Donate

Your home is probably filled with all kinds of things that you and your family aren't using, but that other people or organizations need. Here are some examples of things to donate that you can work with your parents to give:

- Ask neighbors and family members for old towels, extra garbage bags, and rags for animal shelters to use for cleaning.

- Clip coupons to give to a local food bank. Food banks use coupons to get discounts on food they need to stock pantry shelves.

- Give old books to your local library.

- Do you have any birthday or holiday presents that you haven't removed from their boxes? Take unopened gifts—like dolls, games, and other toys —to a children's hospital.

- Check with your vet to see if she might need any of your pet's used items. You may be able to give old collars, leashes, toys, water bowls, or cages to be used by animals staying overnight for surgery or boarding.

- Collect old books and magazines and give them to a local clinic for the waiting room.

How to get others involved

- Speak out. Let people know the who, what, and why of your cause, and how, where, and when they can get involved.

- With a parent's permission, communicate with others about your cause via e-mails or a blog.

- Nothing beats one-on-one interaction. Talk face-to-face to friends and family about the facts, issues, and ways to help.

- Be armed with lots of information. The best way to be an advocate for a cause is to know as much about it as possible. Do lots of research so that you can always try to answer people's questions.

- Be positive. When talking about your cause, point out all the ways that people can make a difference.

- Be passionate. Enthusiasm is inspiring and contagious. Be sure to let people know how important your cause is and how much it means to you.

Raise money

Charity organizations often just need money so that they can keep doing what they do best. There are all kinds of ways to raise money—and have fun doing it, too. Get help from a parent to try a few of these:

- Ask family, friends, and neighbors to sponsor you in a walk-a-thon or a 5K run/ride.

- Organize a yard sale or garage sale and donate your earnings to a special cause. Earn more money by getting neighbors to join in for a block sale. Make a sign to let customers know the money is going to charity. Customers may be more likely to buy and less likely to haggle.

- Sell homemade cookies, cakes, pies, or other sweet treats. See page 11 for a recipe that's easy to make and sweet to sell.

- Work with your principal and fellow students to hold a charity dance or a fun fair to raise funds for a new gym floor or more supplies for art class.

- Hand-make items to sell at a yard sale or rummage sale, an arts-and-crafts fair, a local boutique, or an online store (with help from Mom or Dad). See page 11 for a craft that is sure to bring in some cash. Also, consider raising money to make crafts that you can donate to organizations that might need them. If you sew, think about making baby blankets for premature babies at a local hospital. If you knit, make scarves for disadvantaged families.

Fund-Raiser Make 'n' Sells

Crafty Clothespins

When you're crafty, clothespins aren't just for laundry anymore!

To make:

Trace a flat clothespin onto the back of decorative scrapbook paper and cut out. Cover one side of the clothespin with a layer of glue using a glue stick or a paintbrush and a thin layer of craft glue. Stick on the cut-out paper piece. Let dry. Repeat on the back side of the clothespin.

Make packs of coordinating clothespins by clipping 3 to 5 onto a piece of cardboard and selling for $4 a pack. Include a tip sheet with three ways customers can use the clips, or make a display at your "booth" for customers to see.

1. Coupon Collector: Attach a thin magnet to the back to save a place for savings.
2. Picture Garland: Hang a ribbon on the wall and use the clips to display a set of smiles.
3. Potato Chip Clip: Keep snacks sealed with these cute closers.

Rainbow in a Jar

Make this colorful no-bake craft that is sure to brighten anyone's day!

To make:

Cut a colorful piece of paper to fit on the lid of a clean, small jar. Attach the paper to the lid with double-sided tape. Wash your hands, and open a bag of brightly colored candies. Sort candies by color, and layer them in a jar to make a rainbow. Replace lid tightly. Write a sweet message on a piece of colored paper. Punch a hole in the paper and attach the tag with a ribbon. Sell each jar for $3–$5.

How Can Your Hands Help?

Take our quiz to find out what kind of giving you might be best at.

Circle the answers that best describe you.

1. The animal shelter in your neighborhood needs help. You

   a. grab some pet toys and play with the kittens.
   b. sell candy to help purchase kibble and kitty litter.
   c. collect old yoga mats to help pad animal crates and kennels.
   d. get the word out about when pet adoptions are happening.

2. A family in your neighborhood had a house fire. You

   a. ask Mom to help cook a hot meal to deliver to the family.
   b. collect one-dollar donations to purchase a department store gift card.
   c. give a care package of donated used clothes and toys for the family.
   d. create a poster and hang it up at your local community center letting neighbors know how to help.

3. A boy in your school became really sick with cancer. You

   a. get all your friends together to make him a gigantic card.
   b. give one month's allowance to an organization that helps kids with cancer.
   c. bring him your favorite game to keep him company.
   d. send an e-mail to your friends letting them know the date for the next Find-a-Cure run/walk.

12

4. An old building in your neighborhood is being turned into a community center. You

   a. offer your time to help plant flowers and trees around the building's lot.
   b. sell brownies in a bake sale to raise money for new furniture.
   c. give your old books to the community center reading room.
   d. help the project leaders find out the needs of the neighborhood.

5. You found out that your school is throwing all trash away instead of recycling. You

   a. work with your student council to start a recycling program.
   b. reach out to local businesses to help pay for or donate recycling bins.
   c. donate moving boxes or milk crates to use for recycling bins.
   d. write an article for your school newspaper about recycling.

6. Your elderly neighbor fell outside and broke her hip. You

   a. offer to water her plants until she's well enough to do it herself.
   b. buy some extra groceries for her with help from Mom or Dad.
   c. check out some DVDs from the library for her to watch.
   d. organize a schedule for neighbors to come and help or just visit.

Answers

Hands-on Helper

If you answered **mostly a's,** you like to roll up your sleeves and get to work. You're happy to give your time, effort, skills, and energy to make a difference. There are all kinds of opportunities for you to help right in your own neighborhood. Think about offering to help decorate a library for the holidays, helping a neighbor clip coupons, washing toys for babies and children at a community center nursery, or putting together snack packs for kids in a homeless shelter.

Fabulous Fund-Raiser

If you answered **mostly b's,** a go-getter like you can make things happen. Raising money for a cause is one of the most important things you can do to make a difference. You could sell breakfast muffins to earn money for new computers at your school, or have a craft sale in your driveway to raise funds to help save endangered monk seals.

Donation Dynamo

If you answered **mostly c's,** you're great at figuring out how to get badly needed items to those who need them. Consider collecting clean baby clothes for a local women's shelter or helping wildlife rescuers care for animals by giving used towels or pantry canisters with lids to hold food.

Awesome Advocate

If you answered **mostly d's,** put your great communication skills to work and spread the word about issues that are important to you. Maybe you want to let people know why it's important to turn down thermostats in the winter or keep the curtains closed in the summer. Think about working with an adult to create a blog letting friends and family know how to help the planet and use less energy, create less trash, and so on.

Get Started

Now that you have some ideas for ways you can help others, you're ready to begin lending a hand. Keep in mind that giving comes in lots of different sizes. Serving others isn't about giving the most money or the most time or reaching the most people. It's about making a difference, no matter how little it may seem.

And sometimes giving starts with a little idea that turns into something big.

As you read the following sections in the book, think about all the small things you can do to help that might turn into ways of making a big difference.

Small ideas . . .

- Helping Mom by picking up your room.

- Collecting shoes to donate to a local charity.

- Researching good games to play with your younger cousin.

- Reading to your little brother.

. . . that became BIG

- Getting friends and family together to paint benches at the local park.

- Collecting shoes for a homeless shelter to help dozens of needy families.

- Talking to a congressperson about doing more for children with special needs.

- Reading to kids in a hospital.

Family & Friends

Helping your nearest and dearest

Giving Starts at Home

You don't have to go too far to lend a hand. There are all kinds of opportunities to give back right at home. Helping at home can mean helping with chores or your younger siblings, as well as doing things that bring your family together.

Teach a family member a skill. Teach Grandma the latest step you learned in dance class or show your little brother how to juggle.

Keep an ear out for thoughtful things you can do to make family members feel special. For example, if you overhear that Mom has a big presentation coming up at work, make her a "good luck" card to slip in her purse the morning of the big day.

Help bring the family together by organizing a theme night. Set up a family Game Night, Memory Night, Cookie-Making Night, or Movie Night.

Be responsible for remembering your schedule, keeping track of when you have practice, when a field trip permission form needs to be signed, or when you need to bring in treats for a school party. Create a list or calendar and post it on the refrigerator or computer so that everyone in your family can see it and update it.

Do things before you're asked. If your shoes need to be put away, don't wait for Dad to tell you to move them—just do it. Also, do chores without being asked or reminded. Not only does this help the family, it helps you, too, because Mom and Dad will know you're being responsible and considerate.

Keep your parents informed. Did you empty the milk carton or use the last of the shampoo? Tell Mom or Dad when you use the last of something. Consider creating a list and hanging it on the fridge so that everyone can add items.

Wise Choices

What are all the ways you could help in this kitchen?

Answers:
- Turning off the light saves both energy and money.
- When you're washing the dishes, turn the water off as much as you can between rinsings.
- Organized drawers and cabinets make things easier to find, save time, and look better.
- Don't leave food out—it can spoil, get stale, or attract bugs.
- Help out your parents by being responsible for feeding your pet.
- Household chores are easier when everyone pitches in without being asked.

Pets Are Family, Too!

You can help Fido (and Mom and Dad!) by being a good pet owner.
Help your pets by making sure you do the following things:

- Give them plenty of exercise —even in bad weather.
- Groom them regularly.
- Feed them on time every day.
- Train them.
- Keep their habitat clean.
- Organize their stuff.
- Keep them safe.

By Your Friend's Side

Having friends can make a big difference in your life. Friends can lift your spirits, make you laugh, teach you new things, make events more fun, and share in your wins and losses. Being a good friend is one of the most rewarding ways to give back. That can mean helping her with a school project or organizing her bedroom, letting her know you're on her side, being there for her when she needs to talk, and cheering her up when she's feeling down.

Lend an ear

When a friend is in need, sometimes listening can be the best thing you do. Here are some tips for being a great listener:

- Give your friend your full attention while she's talking to you.

- Let her finish before you speak. Don't interrupt.

- Keep the conversation about her. It's OK to tell her, "I understand how you feel" (if you do!), but don't launch into a story about yourself unless she asks you.

- Meet in person to talk. It's much more personal than over the phone, by e-mail, or by texting.

- Put yourself in her shoes. Think about how you'd feel if you were in her situation, and treat her the way you'd want to be treated.

- Sometimes your friend may cry. Crying in front of other people can be uncomfortable or even embarrassing, but we all do it from time to time. Just let your friend cry and make her feel as though it's totally OK (because it is!). Offer her some tissues, hold her hand, or even give her a hug to let her know you care!

Caring Words

I'm sorry you're feeling sad.

Even though I don't know exactly how you feel, I'm here if you need me.

You are an amazing and wonderful person, and I'm proud to be your friend.

I care about you and what you're going through.

You're not alone. I'm right here with you.

You are really important to me.

I'll always be your friend.

I'm here for you whenever you need me.

I love you.

Cheer her up

- Send her a just-because card in the mail.
- Make her a special craft, such as a bracelet or a framed picture of the two of you.
- Make her favorite dessert or meal and hand-deliver it.
- Invite her over to watch her favorite movie.
- Take her out for ice cream or a smoothie.
- Give her a hug.
- Share a smile by giving her a funny animal poster to hang in her room or locker.

Giving Guide

When a friend needs you by her side, there are so many ways to give her just what she needs in all kinds of situations. Here are some ideas to get you started:

If your friend is in the hospital, you could
- play a game with her.
- bring her supplies for her favorite craft.
- do something special that you know she'll appreciate, such as putting a playlist together of her favorite songs.

If your friend has a family member die, you could
- give her a shoulder to cry on.
- let her know you care by telling her how important she is to you.
- ask your parents to help you make a meal to deliver to her family.

We'll Miss You!

If your friend's parents are getting a divorce, you could
- let her know that you'll always be her friend, no matter what.
- tell her to call you when she needs someone to talk to.
- invite her for a sleepover to help get her mind off things for a little while.

If your friend is moving away, you could
- make a scrapbook full of pictures of the two of you together.
- organize a big going-away party for her with all of your friends.
- work with your parents to make plans to visit during summer vacation.

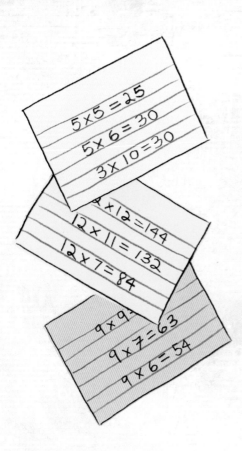

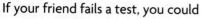

$5 \times 5 = 25$
$5 \times 6 = 30$
$3 \times 10 = 30$

$\times 12 = 144$
$12 \times 11 = 132$
$12 \times 7 = 84$

$9 \times$
$9 \times 7 = 63$
$9 \times 6 = 54$

If your friend fails a test, you could
- offer to help her study for the next one.
- try to cheer her up by telling her a joke or a funny story.
- help her make flash cards so that she can study more easily on her own.

If your friend breaks her leg, you could
- draw a funny doodle on her cast to help her smile.
- help her get around by bringing her crutches, opening doors for her, and assisting her when getting in and out of chairs.
- spend an afternoon playing card games with her.

If your friend didn't make the soccer team or wasn't chosen for the part she wanted in the school play, you could

- invite her to hang out on the day of the big game or night of the play so that she stays busy.
- create a poster that says, "You're my first choice in a friend!"
- teach her a skill from a hobby you enjoy.

If your friend has a fight with her sibling, you could

- listen to her talk about the situation, even if she just needs to vent.
- tell her how you deal when you have arguments with your brother, sister, or other family member.
- give her a big hug.

29

Be a good friend

Other ways you can be a thoughtful pal:

- Help tutor her in a subject she's struggling with.

- Pet-sit when she and her family are on vacation.

- Help her babysit her siblings.

- Help her rehearse her lines for the big play.

- Help her organize or clean her bedroom.

- Help her campaign for the student council election.

- Help her with a project, such as creating a scrapbook for her grandparents.

- Teach her a new skill, such as how to knit or how to French-braid her hair.

- Cheer her on at her next sporting event.

Your turn!
Make a list of more things you could do to help your friends.

GO, ANNA!

30

Do-It-Now Challenge

Lending a hand doesn't need to be a big commitment! You can do all of the following things right now and start giving back immediately. Each idea takes just a few minutes, yet it will make a lasting difference for your family and friends.

- Call your grandmother just to see how she's doing.

- Put away a toy your brother or sister left out.

- Load or unload the dishwasher.

- Slip notes into your family members' coat pockets telling them how much you appreciate them.

- Clean up any doggie waste in your backyard.

- Hang up or put away your clothes.

- Send a friend an e-mail telling her how much you admire her style, smarts, athletic ability, attitude, you name it. Just fill in your own reason.

- Offer to do a chore at home that someone else usually does.

- Whip up a batch of treats to bring to school to share at lunch.

- Fold some laundry and put it away.

- Make a collage poster for your friend using magazine pictures of her favorite bands and singers.

- Clean out a junk drawer.

- Tell your parents you love them.

Sweet Songs for a Friend

I've been singing, writing songs, and playing guitar since I was a little kid. When a family friend introduced me to a four-year-old girl with a rare form of cancer, I knew I wanted to use my voice to help her.

My friend's cancer is called *neuroblastoma* (pronounced nyoor-oh-bla-stoh-muh). It affects the nervous system. If you saw my friend in a crowd, you would never guess she has cancer. She looks like a regular kid and is always so happy and positive, despite her disease.

At this point, there is no known cure and treatment is really expensive, so I raise money and awareness for her by singing at fund-raisers, concerts, malls, and even on the street. In the past couple of years, I've earned thousands of dollars to help her. Although I'll always remember the very first fund-raiser, where I made $101!

During fund-raisers, I also collect "love notes," where people write encouraging thoughts for my friend. These are so great because my friend always gets this huge, bright smile whenever she hears them. You can just tell it makes her whole day. So far we've gotten more than 1,000 love notes. Recently, I wrote my own love note for her—an original song that I wrote about her.

To reach more people, my parents let me post videos online. In them, I talk about my friend's situation, play a song, and give information on how viewers can help. My videos have inspired others, and now there are twenty other fund-raisers going on all over the country to help my friend. And many are being organized by kids just like me.

This experience has been more rewarding than I ever imagined, and I'm so grateful that I've been able to help. I would encourage every girl to give back. You don't have to do what I'm doing to make a difference—just a simple smile can help somebody feel better. Or tell a friend about a cause you're really passionate about and convince her to donate a dollar. Before you know it, little things add up to big things.

—Abby, age 12

Community Caring

Giving back to your neighborhood

Neighborly Ways

Think about all the places in your community that you visit regularly—school, parks, the library, your own yard. Take a look around and you'll see all kinds of things right in your own neighborhood that could use your help.

Challenge:

The local news reported that more and more families don't have enough money for food.

You:

Donate extra canned goods from your own pantry to help hungry families. Or go bigger and hold a food drive among your family, friends, and neighbors.

Stock up your local food pantry

- Decorate grocery bags with fun drawings and scrapbook paper. With your parents' help, drop off the bags at homes of people you know. Attach information about what you are collecting and why, where it will be donated, and when you'll be back to pick up the donation bags.

- Instead of donating food items to a local pantry, give cash. Food pantries can buy much more food for much less than you can. For a $1 donation they can provide up to seven meals! That feeds a lot of hungry people. Ask friends and family for their spare change and let them know how far their pocket money can go!

You:

Organize a cleanup at a neighborhood park, community center, school, or other public location.

Ten steps to organize a cleanup

1. Find a project area and take some "before" pictures.

2. Ask an adult to join you as a leader and make a plan together.

3. Choose a date. Weekends or summer evenings work best for people's schedules and offer the most available daylight.

4. Get the word out with neighborhood flyers and e-mails to friends and family. Include the date, time, and location and how volunteers can sign up to help.

5. Create a plan. Decide what, how, and when you're going to clean. Will you be picking up trash? Raking leaves? Figure out what needs to be done and how you will divide the tasks among volunteers.

6. Gather supplies, such as gloves, trash bags or bins, shovels, rakes, and brooms. Ask volunteers to bring their own tools if you can't find enough.

7. Feed your crew! Have plenty of snacks and beverages on hand for volunteers. Ask local restaurants if they'd be willing to donate food for your event.

8. Arrive early. You and the co-leader should be on-site at least a half hour before the cleanup begins so that you can set up and welcome volunteers.

9. When volunteers arrive, pass out tools, share the schedule, and assign tasks. Announce any additional information, such as where food and restrooms are, and any rules that should be followed.

10. After the event, send thank-you notes to your volunteers. Consider including "before" and "after" pictures to show what they accomplished.

before

after

Challenge:

It's getting harder for kids to cross the main street near school because of all the traffic.

You:

Write to your city council to ask for a stoplight to be installed.

Tips for writing to a politician

Let your voice be heard by writing to local or national leaders. First check with a parent before writing. Then as you write, remember:

- State your purpose. Your letter should be about an issue you care deeply about or a problem you want solved.

- Know your cause. Be sure to research the issue you're writing about. Being armed with information helps you be more convincing. Check to see if any other groups or organizations in your area support your cause and include that information in your letter.

- Locate your **politician.**
  - **City Council:** Contact members about issues going on in your community, such as building new schools, installing playground equipment at the park, or putting in a crosswalk at an intersection. Visit your city government's Web site and look under "contact information" for names and addresses.

- **U.S. Congressperson:** Contact your local congressperson (also known as a "representative") for issues that affect your city or state, like preserving beaches or creating a habitat for field mice. Go to the United States House of Representatives Web site for help at writerep.house.gov.

- **U.S. Senator:** Contact senators about issues that affect your entire state, such as pollution levels. Go to senate.gov and look for the "Contact" button for more information.

- **President:** Contact the President about issues that affect the nation or the world, like helping the poor or creating peace. Send an e-mail to the President using the form at whitehouse.gov/contact.

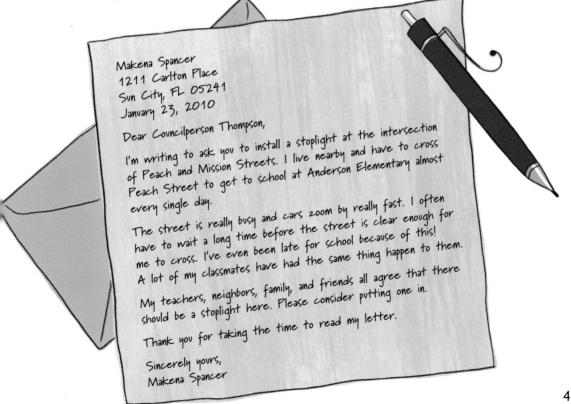

Makena Spancer
1211 Carlton Place
Sun City, FL 05241
January 23, 2010

Dear Councilperson Thompson,

I'm writing to ask you to install a stoplight at the intersection of Peach and Mission Streets. I live nearby and have to cross Peach Street to get to school at Anderson Elementary almost every single day.

The street is really busy and cars zoom by really fast. I often have to wait a long time before the street is clear enough for me to cross. I've even been late for school because of this! A lot of my classmates have had the same thing happen to them.

My teachers, neighbors, family, and friends all agree that there should be a stoplight here. Please consider putting one in.

Thank you for taking the time to read my letter.

Sincerely yours,
Makena Spancer

Holiday and Seasonal Giving

Every day is a great day to give, but there are times throughout the year when extra hands and donations are helpful.

Start of school

When parents don't have a lot of money, their children may not have the school supplies they need to start off the school year right. Collect extra school supplies to donate to schools in your area. Things like backpacks, pencils, erasers, notebooks, paper, binders, and folders are needed most. The schools will help pass out the supplies to students in need.

Want to give something more than pens, pencils, and rulers? Coordinate a backpack drive. Ask friends, neighbors, and members of your scout troop, church group, or sports team to purchase and donate backpacks filled with all kinds of new school supplies. Make it easy for donors by working with your school to put together a shopping list of needed supplies.

Thanksgiving

Spend part of your holiday working with your family members in a soup kitchen feeding the hungry and homeless. You'll make warm holiday memories with your family while helping people who are in need.

If you'll be out of town for turkey day, spend the days and weeks before the holiday raising money and collecting donations to buy turkey and Thanksgiving trimmings to donate to local food pantries. Call first and ask what they need most.

Christmas and Hanukkah

Purchase gifts for a needy family during the holidays. You can usually "adopt" (get teamed up with) a family through community centers, women's shelters, and churches or temples, which often provide a list of items the families need most. If there is not a list, here are a few gift ideas:

- blankets
- socks
- household items
- toys
- family games
- gift cards for grocery or discount stores

If adopting a whole family is too much to handle, consider adopting a grandparent at a local nursing home. Some elderly people do not have any family, which can lead to lonely and gift-less holidays. Brighten their days with handmade gifts delivered in person by you and a parent. Or gather your family members to bring cookies and sing Christmas carols for the nursing home residents in the days leading up to the holidays. Contact the nursing home to make arrangements.

Party Time

If one person can make a difference, imagine the impact a whole group can make! Gather your friends together in the name of giving. You'll have lots of fun, too!

Pet Pal Party

At your next birthday party, ask guests to bring pet supplies in place of gifts. Donate the supplies to a local animal rescue.

5K Run or Walk

Bring friends and family together to participate as a group in a run or walk planned by a charity in your area. Make a fun event out of it by hosting an energy-packed breakfast of fruit, yogurt, and healthy sports bars before the race, and creating team sweatbands or T-shirts to wear.

Fleece Fun

Blankets are great to make and donate, because they can be used by organizations that help pets and sick babies and children. Invite your friends over for a craft party to make hand-tied, no-sew fleece blankets (instructions are on the next page). Ask each person to bring his or her own fleece or work as a group before the party to raise money to buy fleece.

No-Sew Fleece Blanket

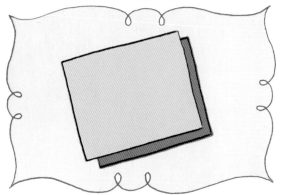

1. Cut two 36-inch squares of fleece fabric—one for the blanket front and one for the blanket back. Layer one square of fleece on top of the other, making sure the sides line up and the right sides of the fabric are facing out.

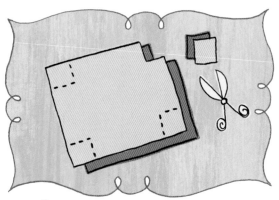

2. Ask a parent to help you cut out a 5-inch square from each corner, cutting through both layers of fleece.

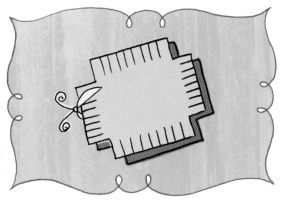

3. Around all four edges of the blanket, cut strips that measure 5 inches by 1 inch.

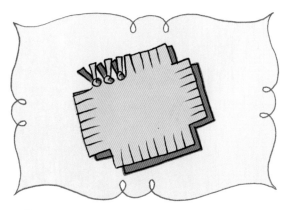

4. Tie one front strip to the back strip using a basic knot. Repeat with all the strips around the blanket, making sure not to pull too tight.

Do-It-Now Challenge

Want to make a difference right now? Take our challenge with these quick random acts of kindness.

- Hold the door open for someone.

- Say thank you when someone holds the door open for you.

- Send a thank-you note to your local librarian—just because.

- Bake cookies for your teacher.

- Share your lunch with someone at school who forgot her lunch money.

- Leave a treat for your mail carrier.

- Smile and say hi to a person at school whom you don't know very well.

- Volunteer to help a young neighbor with homework.

- Take a cart from the parking lot into the store with you.

- Ask your neighbors to help you plant a tree in your neighborhood.

- Sponsor an animal at your local animal shelter (this can be done online in minutes with a parent's help).

- Let someone go ahead of you in the lunch or recess line.

- Give someone an extra turn at tetherball or another playground game.

From Your Community to the World

Many of the causes that are important to you—such as helping animals and fighting hunger—can be tackled by starting in your own neighborhood. But you can also help those same causes around the globe.

Think about the ways you help your community that could lead to helping the world.

Locally

- Raising awareness about helping animals
- Donating canned goods to food drives
- Collecting clothes for the homeless
- Cleaning up a local park
- Raising money for new library books at your school

Globally

- Raising awareness about endangered species
- Feeding hungry children worldwide
- Collecting reading glasses for people who need them
- Cleaning up a neighborhood a country devastated by a hurricane or earthquake
- Raising money to build a school in a poor country

Start at a local level, and then have Mom or Dad help you find worldwide organizations that need your attention.

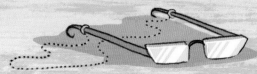

Holiday Helper

This past winter I volunteered at a women's and children's shelter in my community. It's a place where families can eat meals and kids can play. Each holiday season, the shelter turns into a store where moms can pick out donated presents for their kids.

The week before the giveaway, the center starts setting up the store. It was amazing to watch a big, empty room fill up with truckloads of donated toys, games, clothes, books, and kitchen appliances. One man donated over six hundred coats!

Part of my job was putting together gift packages. For example, if the package was for a teenage girl, it would include a variety of things she might like, such as a sweater, a scarf, lotion, and a gift card.

On the day of the giveaway, my job as a volunteer was to take mothers around the store and help them find gifts. One lady I helped had three kids. Even though she didn't speak English well, we were able to communicate just fine, and I helped her pick out some nice presents for her family.

I was really surprised that instead of choosing items for themselves, most of the moms chose items they needed for their homes, such as Crock Pots or sheets. It was really humbling to see what they gave up for their families. Everyone was so grateful for what we were doing, and they were incredibly kind.

This experience had a huge impact on me. I realized how important it is to respect everyone, regardless of their circumstances or how much money they have, and to be very thankful for all that I have.

I also learned that I DO make a difference. While there are many problems that can't be easily fixed, what you can do helps more than you think.

—Milan, age 11

Go Global

Protecting the planet's people and places

How to Start Giving Today

Use the four types of giving you saw at the beginning of this book to help find ways to lend a hand, both locally and globally.

Volunteer

You and your family can volunteer your time by taking a volunteer vacation that focuses on environmental and humanitarian causes. Being a "voluntourist" can be a rewarding and inspiring experience. Not only do you get to travel, but you also get to see the place you're visiting from a totally different perspective than if you lay on the beach the whole time or spent your trip at the amusement park. But don't worry—it's not all work and no play! Most vacation schedules include volunteering for part of the day and activities, tours, or free time the rest of the day.

There are lots of things you can do with your family to help out while on a volunteer vacation, such as these:

• helping with scientific research

• cleaning up an area devastated by a hurricane or earthquake

• tagging endangered plant species

• painting schools in poor regions

• beautifying a national or state park

Even if you don't take a planned volunteer vacation, you can still help out on your next trip.

- Support the local economy by purchasing a backpack at a store in the town you visit and filling it with school supplies. Then donate it to a school that's near your hotel. Hotel employees can help you choose the school.

- Volunteer for a day instead of your entire vacation. There are many programs throughout the world where you can help out for one day, or even a half day. Once you know your destination, do some research with Mom or Dad to find out if there are any opportunities to help out in the area. A good place to start is a nearby state or national park.

- Find out if any of the places you're visiting, such as zoos or museums, need cash donations. You could even collect money to give from friends and family before you leave.

- Even having lunch or dinner in a town's locally owned restaurant is a good way to help a community. You're getting to experience something unique about the region you're visiting, plus you're helping small-business owners!

- Have your parents check to see if there's a river, park, or community center cleanup going on in the area you're visiting during your stay. This is a terrific way to give back as a tourist and also meet people who live in the area.

Raise awareness

Do you have a global cause that you want people to know about? There are tons of ways you can raise awareness about an important issue. For example, if you wanted to save polar bears, you could do some of these things:

- Wear a "Save the Polar Bears" T-shirt.

- Make your next school project about polar bears.

- Put a "Save the Polar Bears" sticker on your bike or a sign on your locker, binder, or backpack.

- Submit an article about polar bears and global warming to your school newspaper or blog.

- Have your parents help you create your own blog or Web site about polar bears.

- Get Mom or Dad to help you make a video about polar bears and show it to friends and family.

- Join a wildlife conservation group at school or in your community and tell them what you know about polar bears.

- Send polar bear greeting cards from a wildlife organization to friends and family. The cards usually have a photo of a polar bear on the front and information on the back. Plus, your purchase money is donated to the cause.

- Rather than receiving birthday gifts, ask for a donation to be made to an organization that helps polar bears.

- Create a booth about polar bears at your school's science fair.

Use these ideas to help raise awareness about ANY cause you're passionate about. But you don't have to do them all at once—just start with one idea at a time and build from there. And just because you're an advocate for one cause doesn't mean you can't believe in or speak out about other issues, too.

Donate

People's homes and belongings can be destroyed by an earthquake, flood, or other catastrophe, so you can really help by donating basic necessities. Find out what's needed by checking the Web sites of relief organizations or by calling local chapters in your area. Here's a list of supplies that are usually requested:

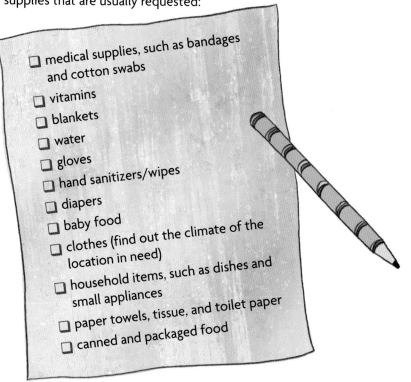

- medical supplies, such as bandages and cotton swabs
- vitamins
- blankets
- water
- gloves
- hand sanitizers/wipes
- diapers
- baby food
- clothes (find out the climate of the location in need)
- household items, such as dishes and small appliances
- paper towels, tissue, and toilet paper
- canned and packaged food

Also, consider giving money to aid organizations to purchase needed supplies rather than donating items. Because aid organizations are experienced in dealing with disasters, they can often get discounts from stores and suppliers. They can make the money you give stretch further, which means they can buy more items and help more people. For fun fund-raising ideas, turn to pages 58 and 59.

Doing your best for a donation drive

When collecting items, think about ways you can gather the most donations. Here are examples:

- Go with Mom or Dad to ask for donations from everyone in your neighborhood, rather than just people you know. By reaching out to people you don't know, you can gather even more supplies. Be sure to introduce yourself and let people know that you're collecting items for a donation drive. Leave a bag plus any information about the drive, and let the person know when you'll be back to pick up the donation bag.

- Have your parents collect donations from their friends and coworkers.

- Ask for donations from friends in your extracurricular activities, such as dance class or any clubs. Be sure to ask parents, teachers, and club leaders, too.

- Talk to local business owners about donating.

- Ask teachers and other school employees if they can help.

- Pair up with an adult to set up a collection booth in front of a local grocery store.

Raise money

There are lots of ways to double your dollars without doubling your work.

- When selling crafts for a charity, get neighbors and local businesses to sponsor you for the number of items sold. That way you earn even more money—from the people buying your crafts and again from the neighbor sponsoring you.

- Use bright, colorful signs to let people know your sale or event benefits a charity. People are often more willing to give if they know it's for a good cause.

- Have Mom or Dad help you get a local business or organization to sponsor your cause. An endorsement from a well-respected group can encourage more people to donate.

- Similarly, get Mom or Dad to help you contact a local celebrity or well-known politician to join your cause. People will often give more if someone famous is involved.

- If you or a friend or family member speaks another language, reach out to people who speak that language. It's a good way to work with people who may be interested in giving but don't know how to help because they don't speak English.

- Sell sets of items that go together. For example, if you're selling cookie dough, consider selling cookie cutters, too.

- Ask local businesses or artists to donate items to sell.

Rewarding and Fun

Volunteering has always been part of my life. I've given back through my church and I'm in 4-H. I also love to sew. So when I was using the Internet and found out about a project to make cloth diapers for babies in Honduras, I thought it sounded like something I should do. I set a goal for myself to donate 100 diapers.

I found instructions online for how to make diapers from T-shirts. Then I asked friends to donate unworn shirts and enlisted my cousins, grandma, and mom to help me. The way you make the diapers is by cutting off the T-shirt sleeves, tri-folding the T-shirt body, and sewing up the edges. I spent a lot of time sewing!

The project took me a year, although I didn't work on it every day. Once I reached my goal of 100 diapers, I asked my church for a small grant to pay for shipping costs to send the diapers to the charity organization, which was in another state. The organization then sent the diapers to moms in Honduras.

While working on the diaper project, I found out about another charity that needed layette kits for babies in poor countries. Layette kits contain basic items moms need to take care of their babies. I applied for donation money through my church to buy needed items. I also asked friends, family, and neighbors to donate baby clothes, blankets, soap, and diaper pins. Then I got help from my 4-H club to assemble and pack 30 kits.

Last year I won an award for my charity efforts. It made me feel good to be recognized, but it feels even better to know I'm really helping people. The best advice I can give if you're thinking of volunteering is to pick something that you can have fun doing.

—Alexandra, age 12

Do-It-Now Challenge

It takes only a few minutes to make a difference. Just try some of these examples!

• Mend an old sweater instead of buying a new one.

• Be a partner to a student who speaks English as a second language. Ask your teacher if there is a student in school who needs help practicing conversations in English.

• Reuse one cup all day rather than getting a new one each time you have a beverage.

• Put away the blow-dryer and let your hair air-dry.

• Share photos digitally instead of printing them out.

• Make a checklist for your house in which you list five ideas from this book and ask everyone in the family to try to do one thing from the list daily.

• Instead of shopping, take your camera to the mall and take silly photos of you and your friends. The pictures—and memories!—will last a lot longer than the clothes you would have purchased.

• With help from your parents, get creative with leftovers and see if you can make up new combinations instead of tossing food that never gets eaten.

• Purchase used clothing, books, or electronics at garage sales and thrift stores. People usually get rid of these items because they've outgrown them, don't need them, or just don't have the space. You'll keep things from ending up in a landfill if they're not purchased, plus you'll save money.

Write to us!

Lend us a hand by sharing how you're giving back! Send letters to

Lend a Hand Editor
American Girl
8400 Fairway Place
Middleton, WI 53562

Photos can't be returned. All comments and suggestions received by American Girl may be used without compensation or acknowledgment.

Here are some other American Girl books you might like:

❏ I read it.

❏ I read it.

❏ I read it.

❏ I read it.

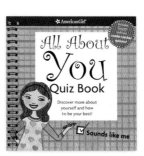

❏ I read it.

This coupon good for a quiet morning.

This coupon good for a hug, anytime, anywhere.

This coupon good for listening.

This coupon good for raking leaves or shoveling snow.

This coupon good for a batch of homemade cookies.

This coupon good for doing the dishes.

When I lend a hand,
it comes from
my heart.